WILDERNESS WISHES!

Tim Emm

ARKANSAS LANDSCAPES

Tim Ernst

To Richard Allen,
Thanks for being
so helpful and gracious,
David Whitchel, ABGCA

CLOUDLAND.NET PUBLISHING

Cave Mountain, Arkansas

www.Cloudland.net

Wild rye grass at sunrise, Buffalo River Wilderness (previous page); Cypress knees, Goose Lake, White River National Wildlife Refuge (facing page)

How glorious a greeting the sun gives the mountains!
~ John Muir

Sunrise over the Ponca Wilderness Area from Firetower Road

All the images in this book are available as fine art canvas or traditional prints in a variety of sizes and prices.
They are printed one at a time per your order by Tim Ernst.
Visit our web sites for all the details, and to view other online galleries of Tim's work:
(www.Cloudland.net or www.BuffaloRiverGallery.com).

Autographed copies of this book may be ordered direct from Tim Ernst:

CLOUDLAND.NET PUBLISHING
HC 33, 50–A
Pettigrew, Arkansas 72752 (Cave Mountain)
870–861–5536
Visit our online store at www.Cloudland.net to see our complete selection
of picture books, guidebooks, screensavers, and fine art prints.

Quantity discounts available, and new dealers are always welcome.

Waterfall on Graves Creek, Big Piney drainage (facing page)

Sunset color, DeGray Lake State Park

CONTENTS

INTRODUCTION

Welcome to my vision of Arkansas landscapes! The word landscape is described as *"all the visible features of an area of countryside or land, often considered in terms of their aesthetic appeal; a picture of natural scenery; wider than it is high."*

This is a new and exciting style of photography for me, and I have worked hard to bring you a collection of interesting and different views of some of my most favorite and special landscape locations in Arkansas. And I took the term "landscape" seriously—all of the images can be considered "landscapes" by the dictionary definition noted above, they are all in the "landscape" (or horizontal) format. And the book itself is a "landscape" format book. I have spent a career of more than 33 years shooting all sorts of wilderness images with no regard to orientation (I love vertical/portrait format scenes), and generally have sought out smaller views and macros instead of wide open landscapes. Shooting nothing but "landscapes" this past year has been challenging, and a great deal of fun!

The images in this collection have never been published in any of my picture books before, and most of them were made specifically for this book. You will find lots of sunrises and sunsets, moonrises and moonsets, cloud scenes, waterfalls, reflections, fields of wildflowers, scenic views, cows and barns and other agricultural elements, plus a treasure trove of other wilderness scenes. There are even a pair of "urban" landscapes included (both depict walking trails so I figured they would be OK). And while they all fall into the general category of the more open-view "landscapes," I have snuck in a couple of "intimate" landscapes as well.

There is a bit of location/subject information included with each photograph, plus you can find more details about each image in the back of the book, along with a few personal notes on photography equipment and technique (I used seven different digital cameras for the images in this book). To read stories about how many of these images were created please visit my online **Cloudland Cabin Journal** at www.Cloudland.net.

There is no particular order to the photographs, and you can open the book and go forwards or backwards at any point. It is best to reserve a block of time though, sit back in a comfortable chair with good lighting, relax and enjoy the incredible natural beauty of our Arkansas landscapes. *Enjoy!*

Tim Ernst at Cloudland
July, 2008

Tim Ernst

Moonset from Flatside Pinnacle, Flatside Wilderness Area, Ouachita National Forest (facing page)

Hold out your hands and feel the luxury of the sunbeams.
~ Helen Keller

Early morning sun and fog at Cloudland, Buffalo River Wilderness (facing page)

Black-eyed Susans carpet the meadow, Rick Evans Grandview Prairie

Reflection along the Cedar Creek Trail, Petit Jean State Park

Big Dam Bridge pedestrian walkway over the Arkansas River, Little Rock

Silvery spleenwort ferns and sandstone bluff, Ozark National Forest

Falling Water Creek, Ozark National Forest

Sunrise at the King's mound, Toltec Mounds State Park

Sunset in Dug Hollow, Upper Buffalo Wilderness Area, Ozark National Forest

Early spring oaks in the pasture, Arkansas River Valley

Fall color reflections on the Buffalo River, Upper Buffalo Wilderness Area, Ozark National Forest

Friendship Falls on Graves Creek, Ozark National Forest

Clouds come floating into my life, no longer to carry rain or usher storms,
but to add color to my sunset sky.
~ Rabindranth Tagore

Hay bales at Steele Creek, Roark Bluff, Buffalo National River (previous page); Sunset clouds and walnut trees, Buffalo River Wilderness (facing page)

Baby clouds being born at Cloudland, Ozark National Forest

Buttercup pasture along Hwy. 16 near Combs

Maple trees at Maplewood Cemetery, Harrison

Sunrise from behind the falls, Dug Hollow, Upper Buffalo Wilderness Area, Ozark National Forest

A forest of "fiddlehead" ferns along the Lost Valley Trail, Buffalo National River

Afternoon thunderheads, Cave Mountain

Cypress swamp, Goose Lake, White River National Wildlife Management Area

Six Finger Falls on Falling Water Creek, Richland Creek Wilderness Area

Fall reflections along the Buffalo River

Slot canyon on Bear Creek, Ozark National Forest

Moonlight in the wilderness, Upper Buffalo Wilderness Area, Ozark National Forest

Sunset and crescent moon along Hwy. 16 near Swain

Time is but the stream I go a-fishin in. I drink at it; but while I drink I see the sandy bottom and detect how shallow it is. Its thin current slides away, but eternity remains.
~ Henry David Thoreau

Heavy snow, Buffalo River Wilderness (previous page); Lick Branch, Ozark National Forest (facing page)

Sunset from Petit Jean Mountain

Pine trees and cows in the mist, Cave Mountain

Summer thunderstorm at Cloudland, Buffalo River Wilderness

Dogwoods and redbuds, Ozark National Forest

"Hoar frost" on a chilly morning in January, Ozark National Forest

Looking down on Hwy. 154 from Petit Jean State Park

Weathered old barn about to fall (it did), along Hwy. 21 near Kingston

Tupelo swamp, Goose Pond Natural Area

Fall reflections and polished river rocks along the Buffalo River

Evening light near Parthenon

Yellow coneflowers, Cherokee Prairie Natural Area

Moonrise, Maumelle Harbor, Lake Maumelle

Climb the mountains and get their good tidings.
Nature's peace will flow into you as sunshine flows into trees.
The winds will blow their own freshness into you, and the storms their energy.
~ John Muir

Frozen cows, Boxley Valley Historic District (previous page); "God Beams" along Scenic 7 National Scenic Byway (facing page)

A meadow full of red clover in bloom, Newton County

Dogwood and maple along Richland Creek, Richland Creek Wilderness Area, Ozark National Forest

The first sunshine of a new day, Frazier Lake, White River National Wildlife Management Area

Sweetgum tree at the base of Roark Bluff, Buffalo National River

Amber waves of grain—a wheat field just outside of Stuttgart

Graves Creek Canyon, Ozark National Forest

Lunar eclipse and old barn, Newton County

Pale purple coneflowers, Baker Prairie Natural Area, Harrison

An infrared view on a hot August afternoon, Scenic 7 National Scenic Byway (infrared turns the trees and grass white)

Wild mountain azaleas and sandstone outcrop, Hawk Hollow, Upper Buffalo Wilderness Area, Ozark National Forest

Oops, I dropped the camera!

Early morning light on the cypress trees, Frazier Lake, White River National Wildlife Refuge

To find the universal elements enough; to find the air and the water exhilarating;
to be refreshed by a morning walk or an evening saunter;
to be thrilled by the moon and stars at night - these are some of the rewards of the simple life.
~ John Burroughs

20,000 snow geese head for the sky, Holla Bend National Wildlife Refuge (previous page); Moonlight and stars at Hawksbill Crag, Buffalo River Wilderness (facing page)

Sunrise catches a bass boat on the run, Lake Dardanelle

Moss-covered sandstone boulders and beech trees in the creek below Pam's Grotto, Ozark National Forest

Backlit dogwood, Sweden Creek Natural Area

Fall reflections at Roark Bluff, Buffalo National River

Yellow coneflowers at sunrise, Cherokee Prairie Natural Area

Spring runoff, Buffalo River, Upper Buffalo Wilderness Area, Ozark National Forest

A lone pine tree looks out across a sea of clouds, Petit Jean State Park

Polished sandstone pebbles at the bottom of the river, Buffalo National River

Predawn color along Cave Mountain Road

Hay bales, Roark Bluff, and star trails at Steele Creek, Buffalo National River (20-minute exposure - the bales and bluff were "painted with light")

Sunrise from inside the big boulders, Petit Jean's Gravesite, Petit Jean State Park

An old barn about to fall down (it did), Boxley Valley Mill Pond

May your trails be crooked, winding, lonesome, dangerous, leading to the most amazing view.
May your mountains rise into and above the clouds.
May your rivers flow without end, meandering through pastoral valleys, where storms come and go as
lightning clangs upon the high crags, where something strange and more beautiful and more full of wonder
than your deepest dreams waits for you beyond the next turning of the canyon walls.
~ Edward Abbey

Pam's Grotto, Ozark National Forest (previous page); Summer thunderstorm at Cloudland, Buffalo River Wilderness (facing page)

Sunset, cypress, and Pinnacle Mountain, on the Little Maumelle River, Pinnacle Mountain State Park

Cossatot Falls, Cossatot River State Park Natural Area

Water hyacinth in bloom just before dawn, Arkansas Post National Memorial

Sandstone boulders and star trails, Big Piney River (20-minute exposure, boulders and gravel bar were painted with light)

A fog bank creeps up the hillside, Ozark National Forest

A mountain stream greets the morning, Ozark National Forest

A spot of sunshine warms up the winter landscape, Kings River Falls Natural Area

Clearing spring storm in Boxley Valley

Cypress knees, Goose Lake, White River National Wildlife Refuge

Weathered barn and starry sky along Hwy. 16 near Boston (painted with light)

Twilight, Lake Harrison walking trail and park, Harrison

Filtered sunshine, Dug Hollow, Upper Buffalo Wilderness Area, Ozark National Forest

Afoot and light-hearted I take to the open road. Healthy, free, the world before me.
The long brown path before me leading wherever I choose.
~ Walt Whitman

Sunrise over the Arkansas River, from Petit Jean's Gravesite, Petit Jean State Park (previous page); Country road in Newton County (facing page)

Backlit maple trees in October (lens zoomed during a long exposure)

Unnamed waterfall along Falling Water Creek, Ozark National Forest

The sun rises over a sea of clouds from Petit Jean's Gravesite, Petit Jean State Park (the Arkansas River is below the clouds)

Moss-covered boulder cascade, Buffalo River Wilderness

Roark Bluff and the Buffalo River at Steele Creek, Buffalo National River

Afternoon clouds at Lake Fayetteville, Fayetteville

Moonrise on Christmas Eve, Cave Mountain

Dogwood blossoms wink for the camera

River reflections, Buffalo National River

Lush pasture along Hwy. 103 near Osage

Fall color along the Ozark Highlands National Scenic Byway (Hwy. 21) near Ozone

A sea of clouds below, sky of clouds above, from the back deck at Cloudland

It seems natural that rocks which have lain under the heavens so long should be gray,
as it were an intermediate color between the heavens and the earth.
The air is the thin paint in which they have been dipped and brushed with the wind.
Water, which is more fluid and like the sky in its nature, is still more like it in color.
Time will make the most discordant materials harmonize.
~ Henry David Thoreau

Polished river stones at Steele Creek, Buffalo National River (previous page); Rock outcrop at Petit Jean's Gravesite, Petit Jean State Park (facing page)

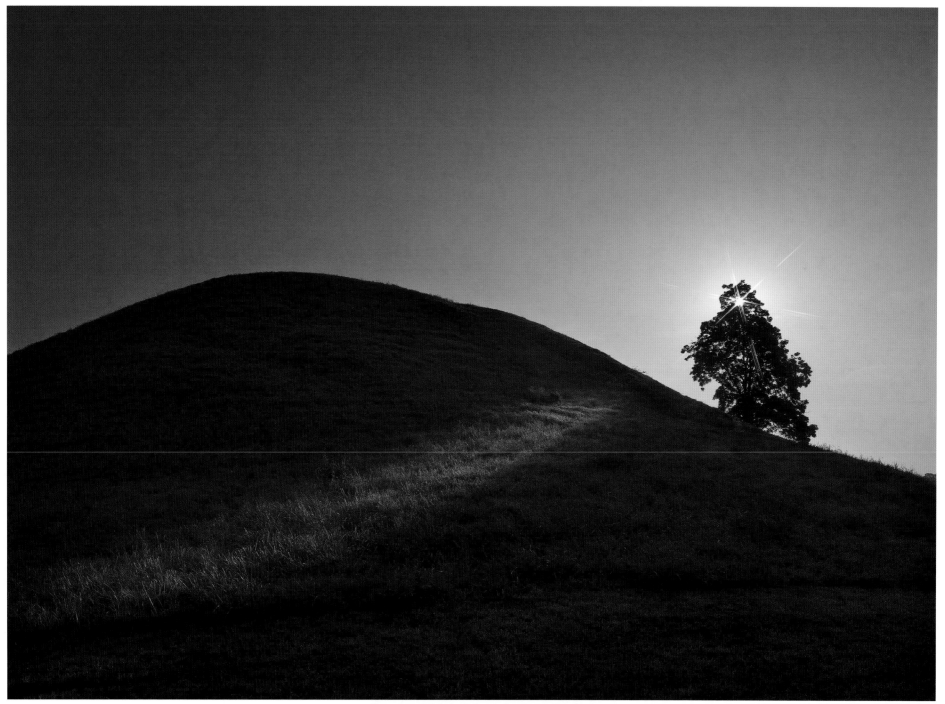

Sunrise, Toltec Mounds State Park

Cedar Falls and sweetgum trees, Petit Jean State Park

Moonset, Boxley Valley Baptist Church and cemetery, Boxley Valley Historic District

Oak trees in the mist, Arkansas River Valley

126

Sunset, DeGray Lake State Park

Wild plum, serviceberry, and red bud, Buffalo National River

Richland Creek, Richland Creek Wilderness Area, Ozark National Forest

A field of daisies blowing in the wind, Grandview Prairie

Cypress swamp, Escronges Lake, White River National Wildlife Refuge

The sun burns through the fog, Newton County

Pinnacle Mountain at sunrise from the Education Pond, Pinnacle Mountain State Park

Bowers Hollow Falls, Upper Buffalo Wilderness Area, Ozark National Forest

Moonrise over the Ponca Wilderness Area from Firetower Road

May you have warm words on a cold evening, a full moon on a dark night, and a smooth road all the way to your door. ~ old Irish blessing

PHOTO NOTES

This new volume of work represents somewhat of a change in shooting style for me. I love photographing macros and discovering the fine details of a scene, shooting verticals, and lots of other types of images that don't really fall into the "landscape" style. What I did here was to step back from my subjects a little more—sometimes just raising the lens up to see what the surrounding forest looked like—all the while remembering to keep the camera in the "landscape" or horizontal format. The images are more open, wider angle views of the world.

As you can see in the listings that follow, I use a variety of digital cameras in my work, from small point-and-shoots to a large medium-format digital camera. My current favorite is a Phase One 39 megapixel system, but I also love to shoot 35mm cameras from Nikon, Canon, and Sony. Over the years I have used 14 or 15 different camera systems, and the one constant is that the brand name on the front does not mean a thing! Technique is far more important than equipment, and I spend a great deal of time perfecting my technique.

The silky smooth look of the waterfall images is made by using a very slow shutter speed of a second or longer (the water moves during this time and blurs). Many other photos here have a soft or dreamy look to them—this is the result of what I call my "double exposure blur" technique where I take two photographs of the same scene, one in focus and one out of focus, then combine them. And you might see my "lightpainting" technique used on a few images—this is where I have illuminated parts of the scene with giant spotlights during a long exposure taken in almost total darkness. The results of all of these techniques are often hit-or-miss, but sometimes the magic happens and I come home with a scene that matches the emotions I felt while standing there.

The most important key to all of this is finding the right light—quality of light will impact the sharpness, color saturation, and mood of any given scene, and can turn a snapshot into a work of fine art. It's all about the light, baby! This light generally happens very early and late in the day so I seldom get much sleep when working on a book project like this. I can always sleep later.

Digital cameras only capture black and white data, and all those 1's and 0's must be processed in the "digital darkroom" before they will make any sense. (I always shoot in the RAW file format.) My goal is to "optimize" an image so that it reflects the scene as I saw it, which might include the mood or other environmental factors.

To learn more about taking great photos, processing digital images, or making fine art prints, come to one of the digital photo workshops that I teach throughout the year. See the schedule at www.Cloudland.net.

By the way, fine art prints on traditional photo paper or special gallery-wrapped canvas prints are available of every image in this book (plus many thousands more).

Page 1, wild rye at sunrise. I photographed this little guy while I was lying on my belly in wet grass on top of a tall bluff. Phase One, 120mm macro lens

Page 3, cypress knees. The tripod was in three feet of water for this shot, and I was watching out for snakes! Nikon D2x, 40mm lens

Page 5, sunrise over Ponca. Had to get up on top of my truck to get this view. My tripod has sharp metal spikes for feet, oops. Phase One, 80mm lens

Page 7, Graves Creek waterfall. One of many beautiful waterfalls in this hidden canyon. Phase One, 35mm lens, polarizer (double exposure blur technique)

Page 8-9, sunset on DeGray Lake. I was back in the water again for this shot—reminds me of the color of the Caribbean. Phase One, 55mm lens

Page 11, moonset. This spot up on Flatside Pinnacle is one of the great sun and moonset locations in Arkansas. Phase One, 210mm lens, polarizer

Page 13, sunburst. We get lots of morning fog around our cabin, and this shot was taken right outside the door. Sometimes I can't get much work done when it looks like this outside. Phase One, 105mm lens

Page 14, fall reflection. The hiking trail goes right under this giant leaning rock. Nikon D2x, 32mm lens

Page 15, prairie wildflowers. This is the largest protected prairie in Arkasnas and comes alive in the spring and summer with miles of color. Nikon D2x, 17mm lens, polarizer

Page 16, ferns. I consider this patch of giant ferns a sacred place and feel like I have to hold my breath while I am there. Shhhhh. Phase One, 28mm lens, polarizer

Page 17, Big Dam Bridge. This is the longest pedestrian bridge in the world (4,226 feet long). Phase One, 80mm lens, cross-star filter, 87 second exposure

Page 18, Falling Water Creek. The water was cold when I took this shot! Phase One, 35mm lens, polarizer

Page 19, Toltec Mounds sunrise. The earthen mounds at this sacred site were constructed according to the alignment of the sun. The king or spiritual leader was thought to have lived on top of this mound. Phase One, 75mm lens

Page 20, Dug Hollow creek. This is a "high dynamic range" image—five different exposures were blended together in order to capture the entire range of bright to dark detail. Phase One, 28mm lens, polarizer

Page 21, spring oak tree & horse. All I needed was a cowboy. Phase One, 90mm lens (double exposure blur technique)

Page 22, Friendship Falls. There wasn't much room back under this low overhang, but I just love to crawl back into places like this. Phase One, 35mm lens, polarizer

Page 23, fall reflections. Good reflections require absolutely no wind. Phase One, 130mm lens, polarizer

Page 24-25, hay bales at Roark Bluff. It was nice of someone to pull back the fog blanket so that we could see this scene! Phase One, 35mm lens, polarizer

Page 27, sunset clouds. I had to run across the field full speed to photograph these vivid colors that didn't last long. Phase One, 55mm lens

Page 28, canyon clouds. This is where baby clouds are born, and they rise up and become adults as sunshine warms the air. Canon 10D, 168mm lens

Page 29, field of buttercups. I'm so glad the cows didn't eat all of these! Phase One, 75mm lens, polarizer

Page 30, behind the waterfall. I always tell my students to point the camera at the sun whenever they can. Phase One, 35mm lens, cross-star filter

Page 31, Maplewood Cemetery. I believe these colorful trees reflect the vibrance and personalities of the folks at rest here. Phase One, 55mm lens, polarizer

Page 32, fiddlehead ferns. I hope it is OK that I included a couple of macro landscapes like this one. Phase One, 120mm macro lens, light tent

Page 33, storm clouds. I photographed this cloud for an hour and the light on the meadow kept changing but the cloud never moved. Phase One, 35mm lens, polarizer

Page 34, Six Finger Falls. This is a very short, but quite scenic waterfall. Phase One, 35mm lens, polarizer

Page 35, Goose Lake cypress. I was standing in waist-deep water for this one! Nikon D2x, 44mm lens

Page 36, fall reflections. I love the way the stones break up the smooth reflections, and then create ones for themselves. Canon 1Ds2, 58mm lens, polarizer

Page 37, slot canyon. I had to lean out over the middle of this narrow canyon to get this shot— it was my first trip to this stunning new waterfall area. Phase One, 28mm lens

Page 38, moonlight clouds. I set up the camera on our back deck late one night when the full moon lit up the clouds below. Phase One, 300mm lens

Page 39, sunset and crescent moon. I was driving home one evening and this scene appeared around the corner. Dumb luck helps. Phase One, 110mm lens

Page 40-41, heavy snow. The landscape had been blanketed with nearly a foot of wet snow when I skied down to Hawksbill Crag to find this scene. Two hours later all the snow had melted from the trees. Phase One, 55mm lens, polarizer

Page 43, Lick Branch. This was the only scene I photographed during a long day of searching—sometimes you only find one, so make it good! Phase One, 90mm lens, polarizer

Page 44, sunset. Sunsets will often create soft hues all around. Nikon D2x, 300mm lens

Page 45, cows and pines and fog. Have you ever tried to herd a cow into position? They don't take directions well, so I had to wait a while here. Phase One, 55mm lens

Page 46, lightning. A long exposure of 30 seconds allowed more than one bolt to be captured. Sony A100, 28mm lens

Page 47, dogwoods and redbuds. Sometimes you can't see the trees because there are so many of them flowering! Phase One, 105mm lens, polarizer

Page 48, hoar frost. When it is really cold and a fog develops, it will often freeze on branches like this. Canon 1Ds, 180mm macro lens, polarizer

Page 49, green highway. Thank goodness not all highways are straight! Nikon D2x, 70mm lens, polarizer

Page 50, barn and fog. This small barn had great personality, but fell over soon after this photo was taken. Canon 20D, 70mm lens (double exposure blur technique)

Page 51, Goose Pond. This is a little-known natural area located right off of the busy interstate near Russellville. It is a great little swamp! Nikon D2x, 48mm, polarizer

Page 52, valley clouds. These little clouds were born along the creek right after a rainstorm. Phase One, 48mm lens, polarizer

Page 53, fall reflections. The white trunks are all sycamore trees gathered around to see themselves in the mirror. Phase One, 75mm lens

Page 54, Maumelle moonrise. The best time to photograph a rising moon is the day before it is full—it will rise almost an hour before sunset when the landscape is still lit by the sun. Phase One, 110mm lens

Page 55, yellow coneflowers. These are such happy flowers! Canon 1Ds2, 180mm macro lens, polarizer (double exposure blur technique)

Page 56-57, frozen cows. I was on my way into town when the sun popped up over the ridge and lit up these chilled cows. They were moving slow. Phase One, 210mm lens, polarizer

Page 59, God beams. I made over 100 images of this scene—the clouds kept moving and so did the beams of light. Phase One, 130mm lens, polarizer

Page 60, red clover. This meadow was made for running through, and so I did. Phase One, 35mm lens, polarizer (double exposure blur technique)

Page 61, fall river. The air was crisp and clear this day, and the colors brilliant. Nikon D2x, 31mm lens

Page 62, painted bluff. Minerals leach out of the rock to create the colorful stains. Phase One, 75mm lens, polarizer

Page 63, swamp sunrise. I was in an inflatable canoe when I turned around and saw this incredible light—it was tough to keep the boat steady. Nikon D2x, 170mm

Page 64, wheat field. This region is known for its rice fields but the wheat fields there are just amazing and go on forever. Phase One, 35mm lens, polarizer

Page 65, Graves Creek Canyon. This is the beginning of one of the most scenic narrow canyons in Arkansas. Phase One, 35mm lens, blue-gold polarizer

Page 66, prairie coneflowers. A prairie wilderness right in the middle of town! Nikon D2x, 55mm lens

Page 67, lunar eclipse. I got this shot by accident while driving home, dejected, after some low clouds blocked the moonrise scene I had wanted. You never know when that great photo opportunity is going to happen. Nikon D2x, 175mm lens, polarizer

Page 68, wild azaleas. These beautiful bushes like to grow along the tops of bluffs, and are often difficult to photograph. Phase One, 35mm lens, polarizer (double exposure blur technique)

Page 69, infrared highway and clouds. An infrared camera makes a striking landscape out of the ordinary. Canon 10D (converted to IR), 17mm lens

Page 70, forest blur. I was playing around by moving the camera during long exposures and found this abstract image delightful. Sony A100, 16mm lens, long exposure

Page 71, swamp sunrise. Get out on the water for the best swamp photos. Nikon D2x, 110mm lens, polarizer

Page 72-73, snow geese. The problem with being so close to a big flock like this is when they fly overhead—you often get goose poop on your lens! Canon 1Ds2, 500mm lens

Page 75, Hawksbill Crag. This is one of my most favorite photographs of all time, and was the last one made for this book just a few days before we went to press. Normally the rock outcrop would have been very dark, so I used a single 2-million candlepower spotlight to light up the Crag. Phase One, 35mm lens

Page 76, mossy boulders. The big boulders give the creek somewhere to play. Nikon D2x, 20mm lens, polarizer

Page 77, bass boat sunrise. I stopped along the highway when I saw a red glow on the horizon—the bass boat sped by right on cue. Nikon D2x, 82mm lens

Page 78, Roark Bluff reflections. Reflections like this have an emotional effect on me—I tend to slow down, be quiet, and even whisper to myself. I will often even hold my breath during the exposure. Phase One, 75mm lens (double exposure blur technique)

Page 79, backlit dogwood blooms. Always look up, you might find something beautiful. Nikon D2x, 70mm macro lens, polarizer

Page 80, coneflower sunrise. I left our cabin early and drove for two and a half hours hoping to get this scene, and I got lucky. Canon 1Ds2, 35mm Zeiss lens

Page 81, wide river. I made this photograph at high noon, something I almost never do since the light is so harsh then. Phase One, 35mm lens, polarizer

Page 82, lone pine. The sea of clouds helps isolate this lonely pine even more. Nikon D2x, 70mm lens, polarizer

Page 83, polished stones underwater. Clear water and surface ripples created this work of art. Sony R1, 52mm lens

Page 84, green meadow at dawn. I drive by this field often and have taken hundreds of photos there—the scene is always different. Phase One, 55mm lens, polarizer

Page 85, hay bales and Roark Bluff at night. The bluff was lit using a pair of 15-million candlepower spotlights for 12 minutes, then each bale of hay was lit with a single 2-million candlepower spotlight. I bet some of the campers in the nearby campground were wondering if Martians had landed! Phase One, 35mm lens, 989 second exposure

Page 86, sunrise through the rocks. It was a tight squeeze for this view but I love it. Nikon D2x, 17mm lens

Page 87, barn reflection at Mill Pond. This old friend that I had photographed many times over the years was about to collapse when I got to spend a few last quiet moments with it. Canon 1Ds2, 122mm lens (this barn is gone now)

Page 88-89, Pam's Grotto. This unique waterfall was named after my beautiful bride, and is a fitting tribute to her. Phase One, 55mm lens, polarizer

Page 91, lightning and weird light. I am drawn to evil clouds and lightning, hoping they will, in the end, leave me alone. The dark clouds above were moving during this long exposure, but the band of white clouds did not move at all. Sony A100, 16mm lens, 30 second exposure

Page 92, Pinnacle Mountain sunset. This is one of the few places where you can photograph a swamp, a mountain, and a sunset all in the same frame! Nikon D2x, 19mm lens

Page 93, Cossatot Falls. I used a variable neutral density filter set to 6x so that I could get a long exposure in the middle of the day to blur the water for this shot. Phase One, 35mm lens

Page 94, water hyacinth. These invasive plants often take over an entire waterway, but they sure are "purdy." Nikon D2x, 17mm lens, polarizer

Page 95, Big Piney reflection. I used a pair of 2-million candlepower spotlights as my light source—each of the three rocks was about the same size, the far one being nearly 1/4 mile downstream. I had to run around like a crazy man in the dark to get to a different location to spotlight each of the rocks during the long exposure. Phase One, 35mm lens, 1226 second exposure

Page 96, creek sunrise. I like to get low to the water and look up. Phase One, 35mm lens, cross-star filter

Page 97, sea of clouds. I have a confession to make—I don't have a clue where I shot this picture! (but I love the encroaching fog) Canon 1Ds, 40mm lens, polarizer

Page 98, clearing spring storm in Boxley. I was clinging to the side of a small bluff when I took this—that was the only open view. Phase One, 55mm lens, polarizer

Page 99, Kings River Falls. A burst of sunshine lit up the hillside upstream just as I was leaving this location. Phase One, 35mm lens, polarizer

Page 100, cypress knees. This forest of knees is right next to the road and easy to get to, but you have to get all yucky and in muck with them to get a good photo. Nikon D2x, 17mm lens

Page 101, barn and stars. The barn and hay field were lit by a pair of 2-million candlepower spotlights. Sony A100, 16mm lens, 30 second exposure

Page 102, Lake Harrison. A quiet moment reflected at the edge of a busy downtown. Phase One, 35mm lens

Page 103, Dug Hollow. If you listen closely you can still hear my cry—seconds after I shot this photo I smashed a $400 filter on these rocks! Phase One, 28mm lens, polarizer

Page 104-105, sunrise over the Arkansas River. One of the best sunrise locations in this part of the country and easy to get to. Phase One, 35mm lens

Page 107, country road. I see this type of road often in my travels, but never tire of the view, or the journey (or the John Denver song!). Phase One, 110mm lens

Page 108, black and white waterfall. This one is for the greatest black and white landscape photographer of all time, Ansel Adams. Phase One, 35mm lens, polarizer

Page 109, maple zoom. I zoomed the lens during this long exposure, which created the weird light ray patterns in the backlit trees. Sony A100, Zeiss zoom lens

Page 110, sunrise. Oops, sorry, but here is another sunrise taken from this terrific viewpoint—looks like someone pulled the blanket of clouds over everything. Nikon D2x, 30mm lens

Page 111, moss cascade. This was a very steep hillside and the water seems to be racing to get to the river far below. Phase One, 35mm lens, polarizer

Page 112, clouds over Lake Fayetteville. Clouds floating by on a lazy summer day—time to go a fishin'. Phase One, 35mm lens, polarizer

Page 113, Roark Bluff. To reach this view you must climb the hill, then crawl out to the very edge of a narrow fin of rock—nearly a 300' fall if you slip. This is perhaps the most dangerous place I ever photograph, and I vowed this image would be my last from there (getting chicken in my old age). There were several buzzards circling overhead the entire time I was shooting this, hoping for dinner. Phase One, 35mm lens, polarizer

Page 114, Christmas moonrise. We were on our way back from granny's house when I slammed on the brakes, and ran out into the middle of this field with the camera. Sony A100, 80mm lens (double exposure blur technique but I kept the moon sharp)

Page 115, dogwoods. Dogwoods always seem to light up the forest, like they have big smiles on their faces! Phase One, 120mm macro lens, polarizer

Page 116, fall river reflections. Come float downstream with me on a leaf and become part of the reflections. Canon 1Ds2, 70mm lens, polarizer (double exposure blur technique)

Page 117, lush hillside pasture. If I were a cow, I would love this pasture. Phase One, 120mm macro lens, polarizer (double exposure blur technique)

Page 118, Cloudland clouds. This is the view from my office window. The Buffalo River is 700 feet below. Phase One, 55mm lens, polarizer

Page 119, scenic byway. Hwy. 21 is remote and uncrowded, but it can really light up in the fall. Nikon D2x, 55mm lens, polarizer

Page 120-121, river rocks. There is no end to the shapes and colors of the sandstone pebbles that wash out of the hills. Phase One, 120mm macro lens, polarizer

Page 123, Petit Jean rock outcrop. Here is yet another image taken at the Petit Jean Gravesite Lookout—the quality of light there is often terrific. Can you spot the gorilla head? Phase One, 28mm lens, polarizer

Page 124, Cedar Falls. I took four different photos with an extreme wide-angle lens and stitched them together in order to get this view. Canon 20D, 10mm lens

Page 125, Toltec Mounds sunrise. This is the tallest Indian mound in Arkansas. Phase One, 35mm lens

Page 126, Boxley Church moonset. While on my way to someplace else early one morning I drove right past this scene. Something told me to turn around and have a look. When I arrived there were clouds above and I could not see the sky (or the moon). I set up the tripod and began to photograph the delicate hues of the foggy church scene. And then all of a sudden, the clouds above vanished and the moon and sky appeared, making me one happy camper! Patience young grasshopper. Phase One, 90mm lens, polarizer

Page 127, trees in the fog. I'm not sure if the trees are floating in the clouds or it is the other way around? Nikon D2x, 116mm lens

Page 128 flowering trees. These are the first trees to bloom in the spring and bring a great splash of color to the landscape (they smell great too). Phase One, 140mm lens, polarizer (double exposure blur technique)

Page 129, DeGray Lake sunset. Waves lapping against the shore is a great lullaby to put the day to sleep. Phase One, 35mm lens

Page 130, Richland Creek fall color. I was like a kid in a candy store when the fall color peaked with a creek full of water from heavy rains. We almost never get both at the same time! Nikon D2x, 38mm lens, polarizer

Page 131, wildflowers in the wind. I used a long exposure of two seconds while the wind was blowing to show the dancing flowers in action. Phase One, 100mm lens, variable ND filter

Page 132, sunrise through the fog. I was standing there taking photos of the fog and the meadow when all of a sudden I looked up and the yellow ball appeared without a sound. Phase One, 140mm lens

Page 133, cypress trees. I like to call this "Snail" Lake, and it has some of the most interesting gray-barked cypress in the area. Nikon D2x, 140mm lens

Page 134, Bowers Hollow Falls. This is one of the most powerful waterfalls in Arkansas—a long tough hike to reach it, but always worth the effort. Phase One, 35mm lens, polarizer

Page 135, Pinnacle Mountain sunrise. This photo was taken recently while I was on assignment for *Rachel Ray Magazine*, and has quickly become one of my most published images ever. Nikon D2x, 17mm lens

Page 136-137, moonrise over Ponca. I took seven vertical images of this scene and stitched them together to make this panoramic format—the fullsize digital file was more than 20 feet wide! Phase One, 210mm lens

Page 143, champion cypress tree. This is the largest living thing in Arkansas, and it took me three days to find it (directions are in the *Arkansas Nature Lover's Guidebook*). You cannot believe how HUGE it really is! Nikon D2x, 24mm lens

Page 144, skunk family. Yup, I'm a stinker for slipping in this non-traditional "landscape" shot! Nikon D2x, 120mm lens

Front cover— see page 126.

Back cover—see page 127.

THE PHOTOGRAPHER

Tim Ernst, 53, lives in a log cabin called Cloudland in the middle of the Buffalo River Wilderness in Newton County, Arkansas, with his wife, Pam, and daughter, Amber.

He has been a professional nature photographer for more than 33 years with images in most of the major nature publications from *National Geographic* on down, including hundreds of national, regional, and local magazines, books and calendars. This is his ninth coffee table picture book. He also has written a couple dozen guidebooks to scenic Arkansas destinations, including the *Arkansas Waterfalls Guidebook, Arkansas Nature Lover's Guide,* and *Arkansas Hiking Trails*. He and Pam own and operate a small publishing business, **Cloudland.net Publishing**, now in its 26th year of operation. Tim also sells fine art prints to businesses and individuals around the country via his online galleries, and through his Buffalo River Gallery location that serves as gallery, digital darkroom, and print studio. And he has been teaching nature photography workshops (which now include digital workflow and fine art printing sessions) to photographers of all skill levels for the past 22 years.

To see or order any of Tim's products, view a schedule of his unique slide programs he gives around the region, get more information about his workshops, or to keep up with life in the wilderness via his *Cloudland Cabin Journal*, visit him on the web at www.Cloudland.net (to view special online galleries of his photography, visit www.BuffaloRiverGallery.com).

Tim with the largest living thing in Arkansas—the champion bald cypress tree, White River National Wildlife Refuge

Momma and baby skunks, Fred Berry Conservation Education Center